SIMÓN BOLÍVAR

LATIN AMERICAN LIBERATOR

FRANK DE VARONA

Consultants:

Dr. Julian Nava
Historian
Former U.S. Ambassador to Mexico

Yolanda Quintanilla-Finley
Teacher and Project Specialist
Corona Unified School District
Corona, California

Hispanic Heritage
The Millbrook Press
Brookfield, Connecticut

Bolívar

Cover photo courtesy of Bettmann

Map by Joe LeMonnier

Photos courtesy of Bettmann: pp. 3, 7, 10, 12, 14,
16, 17, 21, 24, 29; Culver Pictures: pp. 18, 26.

Library of Congress Cataloging-in-Publication Data
De Varona, Frank.
Simón Bolívar : Latin American Liberator / by Frank de Varona.
p.   cm. — (Hispanic heritage)
Summary: Follows the life of Simón Bolívar from his wealthy
childhood in Venezuela to his rise to power as the revolutionary
leader of Spanish-held Latin America.
ISBN 1-56294-278-6 (lib. bdg.)
1. Bolívar, Simón, 1783–1830—Juvenile literature.   2. Heads of
state—South America—Biography—Juvenile literature. [1. Bolívar,
Simón, 1783–1830. 2. Heads of state. 3. South America—History—
Wars of Independence, 1806–1830.] I. Title. II. Series.
F2235.3.D3   1993
980'.02'092—dc20   [B]   92-19459 CIP AC

Published by The Millbrook Press
2 Old New Milford Road
Brookfield, Connecticut 06804

SIMÓN BOLÍVAR

JAMAICA (British)

Kingston   HAITI (French)

CARIBBEAN SEA

PANAMA
(becomes part of
Colombia 1821)

Cartagena

Carabobo 1821

NEW GRANADA
(independent 1819)

Caracas

Pichincha 1822

Boyacá 1819

Bogotá

Angostura

G R A N   C O L O M B I A

Quito

(1 8 1 9 - 1 8 3 0)

VENEZUELA
(independent 1819;
secedes 1830)

QUITO (independent
1819; secedes and
named Ecuador
1830)

PERU
(independent 1824)

Junín 1824

Lima

Ayacucho 1824

Cuzco

BRAZIL (Portuguese)

*PACIFIC
OCEAN*

La Paz

UPPER PERU
(independent 1825
and named Bolivia)

CHILE

*ATLANTIC
OCEAN*

Simón Bolívar
El Libertador

● City

✕ Battle

→ Campaigns of
Bolívar 1819-1825

On a hot, sticky evening in August 1805, Simón Bolívar and Simón Rodríguez climbed a hill called the Monte Sacro at the edge of Rome. The dark-haired Bolívar was strong and quick even though he was thin and not very tall. Rodríguez was the older of the two. He had a long, bony face, and his eyes were sharp and intelligent. The younger man's eyes were lit by the fire of his imagination.

When they reached the top of the hill, they sat down to breathe the fresh air and to look back at the beautiful old city that lay below them in the half-light of dusk. The two Simóns were on a walking tour of Italy. They had known each other for many years. Rodríguez had been Bolívar's private teacher in Caracas, Venezuela.

Back then, Venezuela and many other territories in the New World were owned by Spain. Rodríguez had taught his student that it was wrong for Spain, a European country that lay across the Atlantic Ocean, to rule the South American land of Venezuela. The king of Spain did nothing to help the people who lived there. Rodríguez wanted Venezuelans to be free and to rule their own country.

The twenty-two-year-old Bolívar had not forgotten his teacher's lessons. He dreamed of a day when his country would be free from Spanish rule. That summer night on the Monte Sacro, as the lights of Rome danced before Bolívar's eyes, he saw his dream so clearly that it seemed he could touch it.

He fell to his knees and made a serious promise. "I swear before you, I swear before the god of my fathers . . . that I shall not rest until I have broken the chains that oppress us [keep us down]." It would take many years and thousands of lives before that dream came true.

BIRTH OF A REVOLUTIONARY · In Caracas on the morning of July 24, 1783, rain was running down the cobblestone streets and forming puddles throughout the city. During the rainstorm, a servant left a beautiful mansion near the center of the city and went from house to house spreading the news that a boy had been born to the Bolívar family. A week after his birth, the baby boy was baptized into the Catholic faith and named Simón José Antonio de la Santísima Trinidad de Bolívar y Palacios—in short, Simón.

Caracas, the capital of Venezuela, was near the northern coast of South America, about 6 miles (9 kilo-

The Bolívar family home in Caracas, Venezuela.

meters) from the Caribbean Sea. But the real capital of Venezuela was in Madrid, Spain. That was where the king of Spain, Charles IV, lived. He was in charge of the people who, like Simón, had been born in the Spanish colony of Venezuela.

At that time Spain controlled a great empire in the Americas, which stretched from Florida to what is now the southwestern United States and from Mexico to the southernmost tip of Latin America.

The Bolívars were Creoles, people born of Spanish parents in the Americas. Simón's family owned many homes, huge farms and ranches, several copper mines, and large herds of cattle. When Colonel Juan Vicente Bolívar married Doña María de la Concepción, in 1773, he was forty-seven years old, and she was only fifteen. They had four children: María Antonia, Juana María, Juan Vicente, and Simón, who was the youngest.

Even though the Bolívar family was very wealthy and well respected, because they were Creoles they could not serve in high positions in the government or the military. These important jobs were given to people born in Spain. Many Creoles questioned whether Spain had the right to keep them from ruling their own country.

A YOUNG ORPHAN · When Simón was not yet three years old, his father died. Esteban Palacios, Doña Concepción's younger brother, came often to visit the now fatherless Bolívar family. Simón loved his uncle, who was also his godfather. Together they would go to the family hacienda, or ranch, in San Mateo. Simón loved horses, and he became an excellent rider.

Several years later, Simón's mother developed a bad cough and a high fever. Two weeks before Simón's ninth birthday, Doña Concepción died. Now the four children had lost both their parents. Simón's sisters married, and he and his brother were sent to different relatives' homes.

Simón was taken in by his mother's older brother, Carlos Palacios. He was a cold, distant man whose home was very stiff and formal. Simón missed his brother and sisters, and he missed his uncle Esteban, who had gone to live in Spain. Most of all, he missed his mother.

SCHOOLING · Like almost all wealthy children of his day, Simón was taught by private tutors at home. All of them were old monks from the Catholic Church. Simón thought his teachers and their lessons were dry and boring.

Then, when Simón was eleven years old, his uncle hired a new teacher named Simón Rodríguez. He was a young man bursting with energy and exciting new ideas. He took one look at the old-fashioned books that the monks had given his new student to read and threw them away. The two Simóns formed a friendship that would last for life.

Rodríguez knew Simón was very intelligent. He brought the child a new world: the world of ideas. Rodríguez admired the French Revolution. He taught Simón about democracy and about justice, liberty, and equality. Together they read French writers such as Jean-Jacques Rousseau who questioned the right of kings and queens to rule over other people.

In this woodcut, Spaniards torture an Indian in New Granada. In general, the Spanish did not respect the rights of Indians.

Rodríguez told Simón to look around him at all the injustice in Venezuela. He taught him that it was wrong to treat American Indians so badly and to keep black people as slaves. He also told his student the history of Spain's conquest of Latin America.

The teacher took his eager student on long walks through the countryside. Together they climbed mountains and explored the grass-covered valleys of Venezuela. Rodríguez taught Simón how to stay alive in the wilderness, a lesson that would be very useful to the future general.

Many years later, at the peak of his glory, Simón Bolívar wrote to Rodríguez: "You have molded my heart for liberty and justice, for the great and the beautiful . . . You cannot imagine how deeply your lessons impressed themselves into my heart."

TO EUROPE · Upper-class young Creoles were often sent to Spain to continue their education. In 1799, at the age of fifteen, Simón was thrilled to be sent to live with his uncle Esteban in Madrid.

In the Spanish capital, he studied mathematics and learned French, Italian, and some English. He visited art museums and went to the theater. And he read everything he could get his hands on.

As a wealthy young man from a well-known family, he was invited to the Royal Palace and to many elegant parties and banquets. He was an excellent athlete with a handsome, tanned face and a gift for conversation. He loved to stay up through the night dancing and chatting with his many new friends. He seemed to have totally forgotten the revolutionary ideas of his former teacher.

Then one day, Simón played a game of badminton with Ferdinand, King Charles IV's oldest son. Simón served the ball straight at his royal head, so that Ferdinand had to duck to avoid being hit. The haughty young prince was furious. He challenged Simón to a duel. The queen stepped between them before Simón had a chance to accept. But Simón had shown the world what he thought about Ferdinand, the future king of Spain.

Goya's painting of Ferdinand, future king of Spain.

At the age of seventeen, Simón fell in love with a young woman named María Teresa Rodríguez de Toro. She was a tall, slim, black-haired woman of great beauty. In María Teresa, Simón Bolívar found all the love he had missed since his mother's death. They married in the summer of 1802. He was about to turn nineteen, and she was twenty-two.

The couple went to live at the Bolívar estate in San Mateo. Bolívar had never been so happy. But then, after only eight months of marriage, María Teresa fell very sick with yellow fever. In January 1803, she died.

Bolívar was torn apart by sadness. Later he told a friend: "I loved my wife dearly and her death made me swear that I would never marry again." And true to his word, he never did.

MADRID, PARIS, VIENNA, ROME · Simón Bolívar could not sit still at San Mateo with his memories. He decided to return to Europe. After a sad meeting with María Teresa's father in Madrid, he left for Paris, the capital of France.

The city was filled with excitement. Napoleon Bonaparte, the ruler of France, had decided to make himself emperor. In 1804, he was crowned emperor by the pope, the head of the Roman Catholic Church. Bolívar admired Napoleon because he was an ordinary per-

Napoleon in his coronation robes by Jacques Louis David.

son who had the courage to rise to the very top. But when Napoleon made himself emperor, Bolívar was angry. He thought that Napoleon was too greedy.

Simón Bolívar thought about the glory that would one day belong to the person who freed South America. But he also understood the danger of using this fame to seek personal power rather than freedom for all people. From then on, his ambition in life would be to achieve both liberty and glory.

Unhappy as Bolívar was with Napoleon, he had a lot of fun in Paris. He met writers, high government officials, generals, and beautiful women. Then, in the summer of 1805, Bolívar met up with his favorite teacher, Rodríguez, who was living in Austria. The two set out with a friend, Fernando de Toro, to walk through Italy with their packs on their backs, sleeping in haystacks and discussing the great European thinkers Voltaire, Rousseau, and Montesquieu. Inspired by his teacher and his reading, Bolívar made his famous promise to free his homeland.

HOME TO REVOLUTION · During the rest of 1805 and 1806, Simón Bolívar traveled in Europe. But finally he began the long trip home. On the way, his ship stopped over for a time at Charleston, South Carolina, in 1807. Bolívar was very impressed by what he saw. He thought of the United States and its democratic system of government as a model for what he would like to see happen in Latin America.

One day, after Bolívar had returned to Caracas, he was invited to a party at the home of the Spanish governor. People took turns toasting the rulers of Spain and the governor. When it was Bolívar's turn, he stood up and said: "I lift my glass for the happiness of the king of Spain. However, I raise it even higher for the freedom of America." An uneasy silence fell on the crowd. The guests were shocked, and the governor was furious. From that day on he watched Bolívar's every move.

In 1806, the year before Bolívar's return to Venezuela, Francisco de Miranda had twice tried to defeat the Spanish rulers of Venezuela. Both revolts had failed. But many Creoles were behind him.

Napoleon demands that Ferdinand VII of Spain give up his crown.

Then, in 1808, Napoleon forced Charles IV, the king of Spain, and his son Ferdinand to turn over the crown of Spain to him. He then made his brother Joseph king of Spain. Now that Spain was ruled by the French, Spain could no longer claim its colonies in the Americas. This was the spark that lighted the wars of independence in the Spanish colonies.

In Caracas, the Creoles made their Spanish rulers step down. They put their own people in charge. Bolívar was made a colonel in the army. He and two other men were then chosen to go to Great Britain and ask the British government in London to help the revolution in Caracas. But Great Britain and Spain were on the same side against Napoleon, so the British did not want to anger Spain. The Venezuelans did not succeed in their mission.

However, while in London, Bolívar met General Francisco de Miranda, the man who had led the earlier revolts in Venezuela. They became good friends and returned to Venezuela together.

In Caracas, Miranda was given command of the army. Together with Bolívar, Miranda worked to convince others to support Venezuelan independence from Spain. A group of men formed the First Congress of Venezuela. Then, on April 19, 1811, this congress declared that Venezuela was now a republic independent from Spain.

The signing of the Venezuelan Declaration of Independence on July 5, 1811.

The Spanish army, or the Royalists, attacked. General Miranda sent Bolívar to command rebel, or Patriot, troops in the city of Puerto Cabello. But a traitor there freed captured enemy soldiers, and Bolívar lost the city. The Royal army continued to advance. Finally, Miranda was forced to surrender Venezuela to the Spanish in July 1812. He made preparations to get out of Venezuela.

Bolívar and other Patriots were angry that Miranda had given up the fight. They captured him before he could escape. They turned him over to the Spanish, who sent him to prison in Cadiz, Spain.

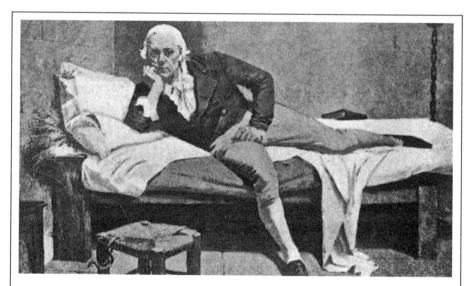

General Francisco Miranda was imprisoned in Cadiz, Spain, where he died in 1816.

Bolívar himself then escaped to Curaçao, an island in the Caribbean Sea. From there he traveled to the city of Cartagena in New Granada (now Colombia), a territory that lay just to the west of Venezuela. He was twenty-nine years old. This was the first of many times when he would be forced to live in exile, outside his homeland.

He did not give up. Instead, he thought long and hard about the reasons for this defeat. Then he wrote down his ideas for the people of New Granada to read. He called upon them to join with the rest of the Patriots to fight for freedom from Spain. He called for unity, and he urged them to attack.

EL LIBERTADOR · When New Granada declared its independence, Bolívar joined its Patriot army as a colonel. He was sent along the Magdalena River with fewer than one hundred soldiers to begin what would later be called "the admirable campaign."

More soldiers joined his army along the way. He captured town after town along the river. Because of his surprising success, he was promoted to brigadier general. Bolívar then received permission from the New Granada government to invade Venezuela. His small army of Patriots captured several Venezuelan cities.

After these military victories, Bolívar issued a famous order called the "War to the Death." In angry words, he demanded the death of the Spanish and all people who did not join the Patriot cause. He wanted everyone to join the fight. The result of his proclamation, though, was that the Spanish and the Venezuelans began killing each other in very cruel ways.

On August 6, 1813, Bolívar's army entered Caracas in triumph. The city council awarded Simón Bolívar the title *El Libertador,* the Liberator of Venezuela. The Second Republic of Venezuela was formed. Then, on January 2, 1814, the Congress voted to give Bolívar total power over both the government and the army. He would be torn between these two roles from this time on.

The war was far from over, though. Royal armies were still in control of other Venezuelan cities. The number of soldiers fighting for Spain had grown, too. The *llaneros,* tough, lawless cowboys who lived in the isolated plains, or *llanos,* of southern Venezuela, had gone over to the Royalist side. They did not trust the wealthy Creoles led by the likes of Bolívar.

A cruel and powerful Spaniard, José Tomás Boves, led the *llaneros* into battle. Slaves and poor people also joined his army. The fighting grew even more brutal. In June 1814, Bolívar fought Boves on the Bolívar family's San Mateo estate. Bolívar's men were forced to retreat. Sixty Patriot prisoners of war were shot the next day. Boves then had the magnificent Bolívar mansion burned to the ground.

*In 1813, after two years of fighting, Bolívar and
his troops freed Venezuela from Spain. From then on,
Simón Bolívar would be known as* El Libertador.

The Patriot army continued to suffer defeat after defeat. In one of the last battles of the campaign, Boves was killed. But Bolívar had already been defeated. Once again, Spain had taken control.

By late 1814, Bolívar was forced to leave Venezuela for the second time. After a short stay in New Granada, he left for Jamaica, a British island and colony in the Caribbean Sea.

LA GRAN COLOMBIA · Bolívar arrived in Kingston, Jamaica, in the spring of 1815. These were hard times for the Patriots. In Europe, Napoleon had been defeated by the European armies. Ferdinand VII, who was now king of Spain, was determined to win back the Spanish colonies in South America.

The king sent General Pablo Morillo from Spain with an army of 11,000 soldiers to attack the Patriots. Soon Morillo had reconquered most of the Spanish colonies, including Venezuela and New Granada.

While in exile, Bolívar wrote his famous "Letter from Jamaica." This 1815 letter was printed in a Jamaican magazine. In it, Bolívar explained his hopes for the future. "I wish to see the creation in America of the greatest nation in the world," he wrote. He hoped Latin America would become one huge democratic nation, "famous not for its wealth and size, but for its liberty and glory."

Meanwhile, Bolívar's enemies had sent a former slave to stab him. By mistake, the murderer stabbed an officer who was sleeping in the room that Bolívar had just left.

Bolívar no longer felt safe in Jamaica. He went to Haiti, a country of former slaves that had won its freedom from France in 1804. There he was given ships and weapons, and he collected a ragged army of 250 men. In return, Bolívar promised to free the slaves in Venezuela. Even though his expedition failed, he kept his promise. He declared freedom for the Africans who had been slaves under Spanish rule for three hundred years.

The Venezuelans were tired of fighting, and they were scared of the terrible power of the Spanish army. But Bolívar was not ready to quit. In September 1816 he set sail for the mainland again. During all of 1817 and 1818 he pushed himself and his troops as hard as he could. By 1819 he was once again recognized as the supreme commander of the Patriot forces.

In early May 1819, General Bolívar learned that few Spanish soldiers remained in New Granada. He decided to take a great risk. He led his army of 2,100 soldiers west across the flooded plains of Venezuela. The soldiers marched for a week in water up to their waists and sometimes to their chests. After that, the army faced an even greater challenge: the Andes Mountains. It was cold and windy. Many soldiers and horses died in the snowy peaks. But the general led them on.

General Bolívar accepts the surrender of the Spanish general Rodil after the Patriot victory at Boyacá.

At last Bolívar's starved and exhausted army reached New Granada. The Spanish army was taken by surprise. Bolívar's victory at the Battle of Boyacá in August 1819 brought independence to New Granada. Bolívar entered the capital city of Bogotá. He was cheered as their liberator and hero.

Bolívar then returned to Venezuela. In December 1819 the Congress at Angostura set up the new Republic of Colombia, named in honor of Christopher Columbus. It elected the Liberator as president. The new republic was supposed to include New Granada, Venezuela, and Quito (present-day Ecuador). The problem was that most of both Venezuela and Quito were still in Spanish hands.

So General Bolívar went to battle. Finally he defeated the Spanish army at the Battle of Carabobo in June 1821. This battle brought freedom to Venezuela. Seven long years had passed since Bolívar had left Caracas in defeat. The people were wild with joy. They gave parties, banquets, and parades in his honor.

In 1821 a congress elected Bolívar president of the nation now called "La Gran Colombia," the Great Colombia. Venezuela was now part of this larger nation. One of his generals, Francisco de Paula Santander, was elected vice president. The capital remained at Bogotá.

ECUADOR, PERU, BOLIVIA · Now Bolívar turned to Quito. The city of Guayaquil had declared its independence from Spain. But most of Quito was occupied by a Spanish army. The people of Guayaquil had written to Bolívar and to José de San Martín, the liberator of Argentina and Chile, asking for help.

General Bolívar and General Antonio José de Sucre brought their armies south. San Martín sent forces northward. With this help, General Sucre defeated the Spanish at the Battle of Pichincha in 1822. Now Bolívar convinced Quito to join as part of Great Colombia.

On August 6, 1824, Bolívar's troops defeated the Spanish in the Battle of Junín.

Bolívar and Sucre next brought their armies to Peru and Upper Peru. The Spanish were defeated at the battles of Junín in August 1824 and Ayacucho in December 1824. All of South America was free from Spanish control. Upper Peru changed its name to Bolivia, in honor of its liberator, Bolívar.

At long last, the wars for independence were over. Simón Bolívar had led the forces that brought liberty to six present-day countries: Venezuela, Colombia, Panama (at that time, part of Colombia), Ecuador, Peru, and Bolivia. After twelve long years of war and death, Simón Bolívar had fulfilled the promise he had made in his youth.

Just when this violent chapter in his life seemed about to close, though, another more personal chapter opened up. He fell deeply in love with a woman for the first time since the death of his wife.

She was the beautiful Manuela Sáenz de Thorne, a very different kind of woman than Bolívar's first love. Manuela could ride a horse, use a sword, and shoot a gun. She was more than physically strong, too. She was one of the few people who would stand up to the commanding Bolívar and tell him exactly what she thought of his ideas. Bolívar adored her. She would stay with him for the next decade, until the end of his life.

THE LAST BATTLE · This should have been a time of happiness and rest for Simón Bolívar. At the age of forty-three, he was president of five countries: Venezuela, New Granada, Ecuador, Peru, and Bolivia. But the news from Caracas and Bogotá was not good. His dream of a united nation was at risk.

He returned with Manuela Sáenz to Bogotá. There the Liberator worked on a great design for the American continent. He wanted to bring all newly freed American nations together in a great confederation. Bolívar invited Mexico, Chile, Argentina, and the United States to a congress in Panama to discuss his idea for unity. In 1826 the congress met at Panama City. But nothing was accomplished.

Bolívar's final years were not happy. After the failure of the Panama City Congress, civil war broke out in various countries. Bolívar was very tired from his efforts to keep the newly formed countries together. He became depressed, and his health began to suffer.

Then, in September 1828, members of the Colombian Congress who supported Vice President Santander broke into the president's Bogotá home in the middle of the night. They wanted power for themselves. They had come to kill Bolívar. Only the courage of Manuela Sáenz saved his life.

The mob screamed "Viva Santander! Death to Bolívar!" Manuela faced them calmly with sword in hand. She told them that Bolívar was not at home. This gave Bolívar time to jump out a back window. He ran to get help and arrested his enemies. But he let Santander go.

Bolívar slowly gave up on his dream of a unified Great Colombia. People were not ready to join together as he had hoped. He finally stepped down, greatly disappointed, in 1830. His old friend Sucre was elected president of Colombia in his place. But as Sucre was crossing the mountains into Ecuador to settle a dispute there, Santander's followers shot him dead.

Bolívar saw the signs of violence to come. He left Venezuela soon after he resigned as president. He did not invite Manuela Sáenz to go with him, thinking the move to exile was too sad and hard for her to bear. He left alone with no money, no hope, and no support from the people whom he had spent his life trying to free. He was a bitter and heartsick man.

On the way to board a ship to Jamaica, he became very ill. He died on December 17, 1830, of tuberculosis at the age of forty-seven.

Today, Simón Bolívar is not only greatly admired in the countries he liberated, but he is highly respected as a brilliant military commander and political visionary throughout Latin America and the world. A nation, a city, and hundreds of streets and parks are named in his honor.

He was a man of great ambition. No one has fought harder to make a dream come true. Simón Bolívar brought freedom to his people, but he died uncertain that they would be wise enough to keep it.

A statue of the Liberator stands in Caracas, the capital of Venezuela.

IMPORTANT EVENTS IN
THE LIFE OF SIMÓN BOLÍVAR

1783	Simón Bolívar is born on July 24 in Caracas, Venezuela.
1802	Simón Bolívar marries María Teresa Rodríguez de Toro. The following year, she dies of yellow fever in Venezuela.
1811	Simón Bolívar and Francisco de Miranda take part in a revolt against the Spanish. Venezuela declares its independence from Spain.
1813	Bolívar takes Caracas from the Spanish. The city council awards him the title *El Libertador*, the Liberator of Venezuela.
1814	Bolívar is defeated by the Spanish in Venezuela. He flees to New Granada and then on to Jamaica.
1819	Bolívar wins a major victory over the Spanish at the Battle of Boyacá. He is made president of the new Republic of Colombia.
1821	Bolívar wins the Battle of Carabobo, which brings independence to Venezuela. He becomes the president of La Gran Colombia.
1822	Bolívar helps free Quito (now called Ecuador).
1824	Bolívar defeats the Spanish at the battles of Junín and Ayacucho. That frees Peru and Upper Peru (renamed Bolivia in his honor the next year).
1830	Simón Bolívar resigns as president of Colombia. He dies of tuberculosis.

FIND OUT MORE
ABOUT SIMÓN BOLÍVAR

Simón Bolívar by Jan Gleiter. Milwaukee, Wis.: Raintree, 1989.

Simón Bolívar by Dennis Wepman. New York: Chelsea House, 1985.

Simón Bolívar: South American Liberator by Carole Green. Chicago, Ill.: Childrens Press, 1989.

FIND OUT MORE ABOUT
SOME OF THE COUNTRIES
BOLÍVAR FREED

Colombia in Pictures edited by Lerner Publications, Department of Geography Staff. Minneapolis, Minn.: Lerner, 1987.

A Family in Colombia by Peter Jacobsen and Preben Kirstensen. New York: Franklin Watts, 1986.

Take a Trip to Venezuela by Keith Lye. New York: Franklin Watts, 1988.

Venezuela in Pictures edited by Lerner Publications, Department of Geography Staff. Minneapolis, Minn.: Lerner, 1988.

INDEX